What is wrong with Cal. Const. amend.chap.85. § § 221.5 (a)(b)(c)(d)(e)(f)?

(Theses)

By

Terry Virgil

McCall

PRINTED PATTERN

7801

Abstract

In truth this is a real hate crime law that all liberals and democrats, plus those that are in agreement with the liberal, and democrats point of view would just love, for that is what Cal. Const. amend.chap.85. § § 221.5 (a)(b)(c)(d)(e)(f) does tell us, for now Cal. Const. amend.chap.85. § § 221.5 (a)(b)(c)(d)(e)(f) is a law that totally removes U.S.Const.amend.I, the freedom to choose, freedom of choice, all human beings Unalienable Rights, plus this law is more a law to bring in slavery to those that happen to disagree, and is an law of allowing immorality as the new moral, and there will be no more parental rights to govern over their families, and this is also a law that has ended what a family is.

What is wrong with Cal. Const. amend.chap.85. § § 221.5 (a)(b)(c)(d)(e)(f)?

(Theses)

In 2013 the State of California's Cal. Const. amend.chap.85. § § 221.5 (a)(b)(c)(d)(e)(f) is the greatest threat to moral, ethical, a direct violation to freedom of speech found in U.S.Const.amend.I, with this law there is no freedom to have any liberty, justice, and no moral compass, there is no more right to choose, or to make a choice, parents have no parental rights; this law does introduce communism, all forms of slavery, perversion, and is the end of all forms of humanities, for this one law must be removed from the books, for it also promotes all forms of evil.

Introduction:

What is wrong with Cal. Const. amend.chap.85. § § 221.5 (a)(b)(c)(d)(e)(f)?
Is in truth a very good and interesting question that has to be answer by the immoral government legislators with the help of the immoral Governor that signed this into California law, and now is spreading worse than a wild fire across the whole United States of America.

There is just one single problem with those that claim to be transgendered, and the fact is There is just no real hard evidence or proof that can back up their claim to being transgendered in the first place; for the real problem is there is no medical, or any physical evidence that can prove this to be a true fact, in addition there is no legal facts to back up any claim for any human being to even be a transgendered person. This is why the question is where is there any proof, fact, or something to backup one's claim to being a transgendered person or some that was born with the wrong sexual orientation (either a male or a female)? The other question is why liberals, democrats, are and those that like to agree or follow these groups are only going on what is called "hearsay"

Hearsay is in truth just meaningless for it is an opinion without any legal proof, or facts to backup the claim without any hard evidence to back up the claim with. Another words a he said she said type of legal debate, in which will not hold up in a court of law, for a judge will just throw that type of testimony out. Well in truth a liberal judge would allow the lack of evidence or a judge that happens to disagree with the United States Constriction and has no regard for human rights or "Unalienable Rights"

Cal. Const. amend.chap.85. § § 221.5 (a)(b)(c)(d)(e)(f) is a direct violation of U.S.Const.amend.I, U.S. Declaration of Independence, Paragraph 2 (1776). Cal. Const. amend.chap.85. § § 221.5 (a)(b)(c)(d)(e)(f) in §(a) does say all schools must obey, and is a demand on all type of schools whether the school is a home schools, charter schools, choice schools, private schools, church schools, church Sunday schools and any other type of schools that is not mentioned in this paragraph.

The other fact is that a parent[s] (father, mother) does not have any right[s] to how the development of the child[ern] is to be raise, for now the government is the only one that can make that determination how a child[ern] are to raised according to §(a) of Cal. Const. amend.chap.85. § § 221.5 (a)(b)(c)(d)(e)(f). It should be the right[s] of the parent[s] of a child[ern] should be brought up and to determine the direction and development a child[ern] that have been put in charge of them go, plus the child[ern] type and style of education, and not the government.

Under Cal. Const. amend.chap.85. § § 221.5 (a)(b)(c)(d)(e)(f) this law is a law of communism, and a law that comes from a dictator like North Korea, China, Cuba, Russia, or could be a socialism such as England, Canada, Mexico, if these type of nations adopt such laws. The liberals and democrats like this type of law because they can get rid of U.S.Const.amend.I, and U.S. Declaration of Independence, Paragraph 2 (1776); the Governor of the State of California has declared himself as a dictator by signing Cal. Const. amend.chap.85. § § 221.5 (a)(b)(c)(d)(e)(f) into law.

The fact is that the Governor of the State of California is dictating to the people of the California for example a boy is no longer a male, but is a female no matter on just how that boy would feel. Okay the example of using a boy here in this part of the thesis is to be an example, but boys are the primary target used by the liberal[s], democrat[s], and those that would agree with group[s] such as.

In truth if another community in another state or district belonging to the United States of America would also fall under the very same guidelines of dictatorship, communist, or even socialist type of government[s] like Baraboo, Wisconsin as a good example.

Girls can do the very same thing as a boy, but for the sake of another type of argument, the male or boy would be used in this thesis, for the fact there would be over a thousand facts, proofs that does should how wrong it is to say a boy is born with the wrong body by him thinking he should have been born as a girl, and the very same thing as a girl saying she should have been born as a boy. There is no medical proof of this even being done. Even psychology cannot even come up with a fact[s] or any proof[s] that would truth[s] in the claim being born in the wrong body.

It is a liberal[s] or a democrat[s] that would say a boy was born in the wrong body, and should have been born as a girl. They say this without any proof[s] or fact[s] to backup what they are saying or debating about.

There is no proof[s], fact[s], or any truth[s] in a worldview biblical view, whereby God has even made a mistake in determining a gender of a child in their mother's womb, whereby a boy should have been a girl v. being born a boy. This is a liberal worldview again without any proof[s], fact[s], or a truth[s] to even backup the liberal[s] or the democrat[s] worldview whereby they claim God goofed.

It is wrong to see a boy wearing female clothing such as a dress, skirt, undergarments, makeup, or anything that would make him even look like a female, and it is even wrong for parents to try and convince a boy that it is okay to wear female clothing. This is called questionable parenting, whereby the parents is a real bad, and evil parents, because the parents or enforcing the boy to be an immoral human being. Likewise the same would go if child was a girl as well. A immoral parent is a liberal parent and the child should be removed from this type of family environment for the safety of the child and the parents also should declared as unfit parents and declared as a child predator, and sexual predator as well. This is also a case[s] whereby the parents are called as a child molester, and this is a form of child molestation. This type of child molestation is a form of incest.

To tamper with one's gender "sexual **orientation**" is immorality wrong and illegal to do, and unethical to do to any human being especially a child who does not know any better or is in developing stags of their growth, for this is call forced mutilation of a child's body and mind.

No parent[s], government[s],or any other human being has the right to even dictate, or tell a child it is okay to even change their gender "sexual orientation" interfere with the growth and development of the said child, for this is immoral, and unethically, for this is a direct violation of that child's right along with that child's unalienable rights to develop in a normal way shape and form. That child is to be protected by the government[s] from all harm in its development even while it is in their mother's womb. It is the Constitutional right[s] of that child even if the child is in their mother's womb to be guarantee safety from all harm that would come from a liberal[s] or democratic worldview; this would even include all liberal[s] judge[s] that would say otherwise, and not even psychology or even other liberal group[s] can interfere with the way a child is to develop outside or in their mother's womb, for a child must be left to develop on their own with the guaranteed rights that have been given to that child by their Creator.

The fact is all of this has come from the religion worldview of the homosexual, LBGT, gay, crossdresser, psychology, sociology, feminist, liberal[s], communist political groups, socialist political group, and anyone that happens to agree with these type of people or groups or type of government[s]. these are the immoral group[s] and organizations.

Cal. Const. amend.chap.85. § § 221.5 (a)(b)(c)(d)(e)(f) is a direct violation of every Human[s] unalienable right[s] that is guaranteed by the Creator. It is also the very first step to communism, and the State of California has a communist government for having this type of law on their books. It is also a violation of the right to have any tradition marriage between just one man and one woman only, as it is found in the book Virgil T. (2014) "The Defense of Wisconsin Marriage Amendment 2006 (Thesis). In truth Cal. Const. amend.chap.85. § § 221.5 (a)(b)(c)(d)(e)(f) is a law that makes all forms of immorality and everything that is immoral such as sexual immorality like homosexuality, LGBT, cross dressing, gay, same-sex marriage, gender changing, incest, bestiality, including feminist liberality. The point is to tell a boy it is okay to feel that they are a girl is pure immoral, and a fact of immorality development in the boy's growth and development. It is also immorally wrong for a boy to be told these things, or a girl to be told these things.

The government[s] has no right under U.S.Const. amend. I to dictate to any individual[s] on freedom of speech, religion, thought, expression and so forth like Cal. Const. amend.chap.85. § § 221.5 (a)(b)(c)(d)(e)(f) does; for this law does remove U.S.Const.amend.I, plus does set up all types and kind of hate crime if an individual[s] happens to disagree with Cal. Const. amend.chap.85. § § 221.5 (a)(b)(c)(d)(e)(f) and boy's thinking their where born in the wrong body, and includes a girl that thinks the very same way. In addition if an individual[s] happens to disagree with the religion of homosexuality, LGBT, cross dressing, gay, same-sex marriage, gender changing, incest, bestiality, including feminist liberality, or even the liberal[s] and democratic philosophy which is also known as (Communism). These groups listed are to real haters group[s], and hate monger[s], bully[s], by forcing those that disagree with their philosophy to be imprisoned, order not to disagree, or are to be tolerant, and are to diversify to the philosophy that it is okay for a boy to wear girls' clothing, and allow a boy to use the girls bath room, locker room or changing rooms if the boy choses to, or the very same thing for a girl if she wants to do the very same as the boy. The same idea goes if an individual[s] just happens to disagree with the homosexual, LGBT, cross dressing, gay, same-sex marriage, gender changing, incest, bestiality, including feminist liberality, or even the liberal[s] and democratic philosophy which is also known as (Communism).

The Importance The Rule of law:

Reviewing the purpose of why there is a need to have this law overturned and be ruled as an unconstitutional law based on the fact that this law does discriminate, and is a law that promotes immorality and immoral behaviour whereby a boy for example could be faking the idea of a boy saying that he is a girl in order to be in a girls bath room, locker room, or even a female changing room just to spy or look at a females private body parts.

When there is a law that promotes immorality and any immoral behaviour would also promote immoral behaviour such as incest, bestiality, public nudity, and sex in public places, teenage pregnancy, pedophiles, perversion to be legal and a right to be done by every American. This would also mean that everything that is moral would be illegal and wrong to do, plus all morality would be a hate crime. Yet with a law like the Cal.Const. amend.chap.85. § § 221.5 (a)(b)(c)(d)(e)(f) does show that all liberals, democrats and those that like to think that laws like this one are in truth those that would like to have all forms of perversions legal, for one can see it when the Governor Jerry Brown of California signed this law and made it part of the California Constitution. This would be the very first immoral law making immorality and perversions that are immoral legal in the State of California.

In reality the argument that the State of California does have on its side to say that the State of California has every right to make a law like the Cal.Const. amend.chap.85. § § 221.5 (a)(b)(c)(d)(e)(f) legal is to be found in the U.S.Const.amend.X "The powers not delegated to the United States by the Constitution, nor prohibited by it to the states, are reserved to the states respectively, or to the people" This Constitutional Amendment would be the only law[s] that does side with the State of California if Cal.Const. amend.chap.85. § § 221.5 (a)(b)(c)(d)(e)(f) would be challenged in the United States Supreme Court. However would the liberal judges side and uphold Cal.Const. amend.chap.85. § § 221.5 (a)(b)(c)(d)(e)(f) as a legal rights law[s], or would the United States Supreme Court uphold the law based on equal right[s].

Now if other States would just happen to adopt Cal.Const. amend.chap.85. § § 221.5 (a)(b)(c)(d)(e)(f) or even a school district[s] in another state[s] that does not have such law[s] like the Cal.Const. amend.chap.85. § § 221.5 (a)(b)(c)(d)(e)(f) as law[s] or a community[s] in such State[s] even if part of the school district[s] in such state[s] even adopted such law[s]; the question that the United States Supreme Court or the Supreme Court of said State[s] would have to either rule the law[s] as constitutional or strike down the law[s] as being unconstitutional.

Now according to Cal.Const. amend.chap.85. § § 221.5 (a)(b)(c)(d)(e)(f) it is illegal for Churches, church school[s] (Sunday School[s]), parochial school[s],private school[s],home school[s],charter school[s],school choice school[s]to even have a doctrine that would not allow a for example a boy that wants to wear female clothing or to even think that he was to be born a female, and would hold a worldview forbidding a boy from partaking in all the type[s] of school[s] mentioned in this sentence. In addition all conservative Church would be forced under the law[s] to rewrite the Bible (The Word of God) in order to be forced to allow such immoral behaviour of immorality, and all Pastors, Ministers, and Church lay leaders would be forced not to say or preach in their sermons or say anything that would be considered as to be against the idea of boys wearing female clothing or wanting to look like a female by saying it is a sin for a boy to wear female clothing or even to look like a female to help the boy to think they are a female. In truth the Cal.Const. amend.chap.85. § § 221.5 (a)(b)(c)(d)(e)(f) says God is wrong; therefore if the government says that a church must be mandated to preach and teach what the government says it is to teach and preach the church is to obey the government v. what God teaches. In addition the U.S.Const.amend.I would no longer be in existence, but now that this is the law[s] in the State of California that does mean in the State of California there is no such thing as U.S.Const.amend.I anymore and it is illegal to protest against Cal.Const. amend.chap.85. § § 221.5 (a)(b)(c)(d)(e)(f) under Cal.Const. amend.chap.85. § § 221.5 (a)(b)(c)(d)(e)(f), for Cal.Const. amend.chap.85. § § 221.5 (a)(b)(c)(d)(e)(f) is the law in the State of California, because U.S.Const.amend.I does not even exist.

As one can see that Governor Jerry Brown and the liberals along with the democrats forgot or are unwilling to review or accept the United States Constitution, or want to accept the United States of America's Constitution as just a living constitution meaning whatever a person feels that United States Constitution means to them instead of the United States Constitution to be a written document.

It is very important to know and understand that the rule of law is not what one thinks it is, for or just a living law[s] like the liberals and democrats would like everyone to think, for the rule of law[s] is a document stating what is legal and what is not legal. Wrong thinking is the being of immorality thinking that whatever is immoral is to be legal, and morality and all moral thinks, ideas, are all illegal. One could say what is right is now wrong and the wrong is now right or one could say well is now evil and evil is now good.

The other part of rule of law[s] is the very question about mutation of the human body; which by the way is not even debated for a very good reason, and that reason is Cal.Const. amend.chap.85. § § 221.5 (a)(b)(c)(d)(e)(f) does make and open the door to allow for example a boy to remove his penis and testicles and have a Virginia in place of those two male body parts, plus a boy would be allowed to develop breast even if the parents disagree with Cal.Const. amend.chap.85. § § 221.5 (a)(b)(c)(d)(e)(f) the mandate would be the government has stripped the parent[s] of the right to have their child develop the way they fell fit. The mandate under Cal.Const. amend.chap.85. § § 221.5 (a)(b)(c)(d)(e)(f) is no to any parent[s] right any more, for the child is the property of the government only; therefore the government is the only one that has a say on how the child in this case as the example of a boy wanting to wear female clothing and to be classified as a female the government and all the courts would have to make a ruling that the boy is no longer a male, but is now a female and live as a female if the boy choose to live as a female, and there cannot be any interference at all by the parent[s] of the child in this case for argument sake a boy; therefore the boy would have the very same rights as a female would under the law[s], and the very same treatment under the law[s].

Under the rule of law[s] the determination of one's gender whether one is a male or female is to be determined not by the way a child is in its mother's womb at the time of conception, for at the time of conception is when a child's gender is a male or female and that is determined by the sperm that comes from the child's father; therefore under rule of law[s] in the State of California the gender of the child is to be determined by the child or the government of California. This is part of the mandate under Cal.Const. amend.chap.85. § § 221.5 (a)(b)(c)(d)(e)(f).

To mandate like Cal.Const. amend.chap.85. § § 221.5 (a)(b)(c)(d)(e)(f) does read is a form of communism, well in truth it is communism style and type of government and governing. Another words according to rule of law[s] Governor Jerry Brown has mandated himself as a dictator to the State of California; therefore his rule of law[s] is law[s]. With this in mind all conservatives must obey Governor's Jerry Brown's like those that live in North Korea and their Communism type of government.

Cal.Fam.Code §7500 §(a)(b)(c) "(a) The mother of an unemancipated minor child, and the father, if presumed to be the father under Section 7611, are equally entitled to the services and earnings of the child.(b) If one parent is dead, is unable or refuses to take custody, or has abandoned the child, the other parent is entitled to the services and earnings of the child. (c) This section shall not apply to any services or earnings of an unemancipated minor child related to a contract of a type described in Section 6750."

CAL. Fam. Code. § 7501§(a)(b)" (a) A parent entitled to the custody of a child has a right to change the residence of the child, subject to the power of the court to restrain a removal that would prejudice the rights or welfare of the child.(b) It is the intent of the Legislature to affirm the decision in In re Marriage of Burgess (1996) 13 Cal.4th 25, and to declare that ruling to be the public policy and law of this state."

Cal.Fam.Code. § 7002 "The parent, as such, has no control over the property of the child"

State of California Head of Household (HOH) Legal Definitions under Qualifying Child https://www.ftb.ca.gov/individuals/hoh/selftest/definitions.shtml#ParentStepparent "A qualifying child is a person who meets all of the following tests: relationship test. The person must be one of the relatives listed below or a descendant of such a person. birth child, stepchild, brother, half-brother, stepbrother, nephew, eligible foster child, grandchild, adopted child, sister, half-sister, stepsister, niece" Seeing that the test does prove that a child is the responsibility and a parent[s] are to held accountable for any and all children that is in their care either placed in their care by law or a legal adoption or legal foster care. Now according to this definition and it is a tax code the state of California would even violate it very own law by saying it is okay for a boy as an example to even wear a dress or have his gender (sexual organization) as it is real called changed by the government if the parent[s] happen to object to having their son be a girl in any case and the parent[s] have the right to even object to their son to wear a dress and act like a girl if the boy wishes. This one fact has to be truth that the state of California has got to remove the boy form the custody of his parent[s] then declare the boy to no longer have the identification that identifies him as a male, then the State of California must change all of his identification and declare him as a female, plus the State of California must force the said boy to have his gender (sexual organization) changed to whereby he will have to live the rest of his natural life as a female so that he would be incompliance to Cal.Const. amend.chap.85. § § 221.5

14

(a)(b)(c)(d)(e)(f), and in addition the State of California is now the parent of the said "boy" in question and the State of California is to be held both accountable, and is now responsible of the welfare of the said" boy" now said "girl" ; therefore the State of California must provide clothing that the now girl has to wear, and provide an education, and is to be held both accountable and responsible for the safety of the said "child"; therefore if the said "child" is bullied, or anything that is not covered here in this thesis, in truth the State of California along with Governor Jerry Brown can be charged with neglect of the said "child" and can be punished according to the law[s] and codes of the State of California. In addition both the State of California and Governor Jerry Brown can be sued for mutation of a child. All of this would be the rule of law and is the true definition of rule of law according to the Cal.Const. amend.chap.85. § § 221.5 (a)(b)(c)(d)(e)(f) and the California's Constitution.

There is a huge conflict of rule of law between Cal.Const. amend.chap.85. § § 221.5 (a)(b)(c)(d)(e)(f) and California' tax codes that happen to identify just what a family is plus what is the rights of a parent[s] in the case of the development of a child that happens to be also found in California's family law[s]. The equal rights violation would be the fact that all liberal law[s] such as Cal.Const. amend.chap.85. § § 221.5 (a)(b)(c)(d)(e)(f) is a direct violation of human right that are also found in U.S. Declaration of Independence, Paragraph 2 (1776) "We hold these truths to be self-evident, that all men are created equal, that they are endowed by their Creator with certain unalienable Rights, that among these are Life, Liberty and the pursuit of Happiness.--That to secure these rights, Governments are instituted among Men, deriving their just powers from the consent of the governed, --That whenever any Form of Government becomes destructive of these ends, it is the Right of the People to alter or to abolish it, and to institute new Government, laying its foundation on such principles and organizing its powers in such form, as

15

to them shall seem most likely to effect their Safety and Happiness. Prudence, indeed, will dictate that Governments long established should not be changed for light and transient causes; and accordingly all experience hath shewn, that mankind are more disposed to suffer, while evils are sufferable, than to right themselves by abolishing the forms to which they are accustomed. But when a long train of abuses and usurpations, pursuing invariably the same Object evinces a design to reduce them under absolute Despotism, it is their right, it is their duty, to throw off such Government, and to provide new Guards for their future security.--Such has been the patient sufferance of these Colonies; and such is now the necessity which constrains them to alter their former Systems of Government. The history of the present King of Great Britain is a history of repeated injuries and usurpations, all having in direct object the establishment of an absolute Tyranny over these States. To prove this, let Facts be submitted to a candid world."

The direct violation and words that must be looked at are these words "We hold these truths to be self-evident, that all men are created equal, that they are endowed by their Creator with certain unalienable Rights, that among these are Life, Liberty and the pursuit of Happiness.--That to secure these rights". This too must be held as rule of law and the State of California must obey such law[s], for it is a direct violation of human and parental rights according to the U.S. Declaration of Independence, Paragraph 2 (1776).

What is wrong with Cal.Const. amend.chap.85. § § 221.5 (a)(b)(c)(d)(e)(f)

After looking at the rule of law, and yes the State of California has the right to have a law[s] as long as the State of California can exercise their constitutional right that are found U.S.Const.amend.X because the State of California does have the right to make its own law[s], but there are several things that are so very wrong with Cal.Const. amend.chap.85. § § 221.5 (a)(b)(c)(d)(e)(f), for the fact there is no right[s] for a parent to develop, and raise their child as their own, for where are the parental right[s], and there is no freedom to be free, plus all liberty is no longer in the State of California. Without any of these Unalienable Rights the parent has no right to raise or develop a child that is put in their custody by God Himself, for it is God and God alone that grant all parent[s] the free will to raise and develop a child as they feel fit whether the parent[s] believe in God or not. This is the freedom that comes from God. this is the point that is written and meaning that comes from the U.S. Declaration of Independence, Paragraph 2 (1776) "We hold these truths to be self-evident, that all men are created equal, that they are endowed by their Creator with certain unalienable Rights, that among these are Life, Liberty and the pursuit of Happiness"

As it is written in the U.S. Declaration of Independence, Paragraph 2 (1776) to be a parent means that you have certain unalienable rights to raise, and develop a child, and it is not the right[s] of the government to tell, dictate, or even mandate how a parent[s] are to raise and develop their child that has been place in their care by God.

The biggest problem is that a law[s] like Cal.Const. amend.chap.85. § § 221.5 (a)(b)(c)(d)(e)(f) are in truth law[s] that come from the communist type of government or is also known as big government like all liberals and democrats would like to have and see, for a law like Cal.Const. amend.chap.85. § § 221.5 (a)(b)(c)(d)(e)(f) is communism and a law that is not freedom or having any liberty like the liberals and democrats, because all liberals and democrat just hate the idea of having freedom to be free and to have liberty too. California's governor Jerry Brown is the real proof that this is the fact that he does not like freedom to be free and to have liberty for the legal citizens of the State of California. Governor Jerry Brown want to have the whole State of California as a communist State so that he can rule as a dictator.

By Governor Jerry Brown of California signing Cal.Const. amend.chap.85. § § 221.5

(a)(b)(c)(d)(e)(f) into law does mean that all legal citizens in the State of California would not have any more U.S.Const.amend.I rights at all.

According to U.S.Const.amend.I "Congress shall make no law respecting an establishment of religion, or prohibiting the free exercise thereof; or abridging the freedom of speech, or of the press; or the right of the people peaceably to assemble, and to petition the government for a redress of grievances." The key words are free exercise, freedom of speech, press and the right of the people to peacefully assemble, and to petition the government for redress of grievance. Now Cal.Const. amend.chap.85. § § 221.5 (a)(b)(c)(d)(e)(f) does remove everything that has been talked or written about, for Governor Jerry Brown of California has established a State religion, for all forms of homosexuality and immorality to be immoral is now an establishment of religion, because for example if a boy feels that he is a girl and want to use girls bath room, locker room or a ladies changing room it would be his religious right to do so because the State of California has established this type of immoral behaviour as a religion.

Cal.Const. amend.chap.85. § § 221.5 (a)(b)(c)(d)(e)(f) is a law of religion making it illegal for an and all types of Pastors, Sunday School teachers, lay-leaders of a church, Minsters, and any other type of church officials to even speak out against this type of immoral behaviour that for example a boy would want to do. It is a freedom of speech that would be violated because of Cal.Const. amend.chap.85. § § 221.5 (a)(b)(c)(d)(e)(f) in the case of a Pastors, Sunday School teachers, lay-leaders of a church, Minsters, and any other type of church officials to even speak out against this type of immoral behaviour, or any other citizen that happens to legal not just in the State of California, but a legal citizen of the United States of America too.

Here is a point that should be well made in history about freedom of religion in the

United States of America and the State of California along with Governor Jerry Brown has forgotten this real reason why freedom of religion is so important and the freedom of speech as well, for if you look at the Mayflower Compact of 1620 you would see these words, Johnson C. (1994-2013) MayflowerHistory.com. Retrieved from http://mayflowerhistory.com/mayflower-compact/ "In ye name of God Amen· We whose names are vnderwriten, the loyall subjects of our dread soueraigne Lord King James by ye grace of God, of great Britaine, franc, & Ireland king, defender of ye faith, &c Haueing vndertaken, for ye glorie of God, and aduancemente of ye christian ^faith and honour of our king & countrie, a voyage to plant ye first colonie in ye Northerne parts of Virginia· doe by these presents solemnly & mutualy in ye presence of God, and one of another, couenant, & combine our selues togeather into a ciuill body politick; for ye our better ordering, & preseruation & fur= therance of ye ends aforesaid; and by vertue hearof, to enacte, constitute, and frame shuch just & equall lawes, ordinances, Acts, constitutions, & offices, from time to time, as shall be thought most meete & conuenient for ye generall good of ye colonie: vnto which we promise all due submission and obedience. In witnes wherof we haue herevnder subscribed our names at Cap=Codd ye ·11· of Nouember, in ye year of ye raigne of our soueraigne Lord king James of England, france, & Ireland ye eighteenth and of Scotland ye fiftie fourth. Ano: Dom ·1620·"|

Signers John Carver, William Bradford, Edward Winslow, William Brewster, Isaac Allerton Myles Standish, John Alden, Samuel Fuller, Christopher Martin, William Mullins, William White, Richard Warren, John Howland, Stephen Hopkins, Edward Tilley, John Tilley, Francis Cooke, Thomas Rogers, Thomas Tinker, John Rigsdale, Edward Fuller, John Turne, Francis Eaton, James Chilton, John Crackstone, John Billington, Moses Fletcher, John Goodman, Degory, Priest Thomas, Williams Gilbert, Winslow Edmund, Margesson Peter Browne, Richard

Britteridge, George Soule, Richard Clarke, Richard Gardiner, John Allerton, Thomas English, Edward Doty, Edward Leister" As history would show that it was religious freedom and to be free wo worship God in one's own way is the real reason why the Pilgrims set forth to the United States of America in order to have the unalienable right[s] and freedom to have the liberty. Not the way the liberals and democrats would have everyone to believe like the liberal democrat Governor Jerry Brown by signing in an anti-freedom law like the Cal.Const. amend.chap.85. § § 221.5 (a)(b)(c)(d)(e)(f).

The "free exercise thereof" is part of the U.S.Const.amend.I is a very important part that tells every legal citizen of the United States of America that it is okay to speak out against law[s] like Cal.Const. amend.chap.85. § § 221.5 (a)(b)(c)(d)(e)(f) or Governors like Governor Jerry Brown of the State of California, or any other Government officials that has directly and willfully violated not just the United States Constitution, or their own States Constitution, but other document like the Mayflower Compact of 1620. This would also mean that the United States Constitution is not a living Constitution like the liberals and democrats like Governor Jerry Brown along with the liberal President Obama and Wisconsin's United States Senator Tammy Baldwin has said in the past, but documents like the Mayflower Compact of 1620, The United States Constitution, and the Declaration of Independence are real and written to be the law of the nation; therefore there is no such thing as a living Constitution at all.

A living constitution does mean whatever one feels and thinks is right or wrong does go and is correct. Not that is the problem with the terminology and words like living law[s].

"Freedom of press" is eliminated because the press would not be able to report anything that is wrong about Cal.Const. amend.chap.85. § § 221.5 (a)(b)(c)(d)(e)(f), for the press would have to be handcuffed to what they can and cannot say, but in the case of a religious group or organization such as a church, then the press would be forced to say the church is a hate group against all forms of immorality and immoral life style like a boy wearing a dress.

"The right of the people to peacefully assemble, and to petition the government for redress of grievance." The Part of U.S.Const.amend.I is meaning less and a part of the United States Constitution that all liberals democrats would like to see removed, for all liberals and democrats like the very same idea as a communist nation would not establish because a communist does not like the words peacefully assemble and to petition for a regress of grievance.

A church is a place for the legal citizens of the United State of America to even assemble and to talk about whatever they feel free to talk about, even if the church feel to talk about why it is against Cal.Const. amend.chap.85. § § 221.5 (a)(b)(c)(d)(e)(f) Governor Jerry Brown of California, President Obama, and even Wisconsin's United States Senator Tammy Baldwin. The right to speak out against all forms of immorality like homosexuality, boy's cross-dressing and so forth.

By the way a church is a private place whereby everyone is welcome to peacefully assemble; therefore the Cal.Const. amend.chap.85. § § 221.5 (a)(b)(c)(d)(e)(f) would force a church to be a public place to assemble whereby the ones holding the assembly or meeting at a church this would include a church worship service whereby it would be illegal to even speak out against the Cal.Const. amend.chap.85. § § 221.5 (a)(b)(c)(d)(e)(f).

In truth Governor Jerry Brown of California could establish an organization or a law enforcement agency to enforce a law[s] that would prevent a church or anyone that is a legal citizen that would say anything against the immoral and immorality of homosexuality, or a boy that would want to even wear girls' clothing, or anything a classify anything such as speaking out as a hate crime or bulling those boys' for example that want to wear girls' clothing if they wish.

The door has been open to the fact that Governor Jerry Brown of California signed Cal.Const. amend.chap.85. § § 221.5 (a)(b)(c)(d)(e)(f) to boys that want to be dressed as a girl to be bullied, and all kind of discrimination and harassment and all other type of ridicule. It is also the fact that Governor Jerry Brown of California has discriminated against those that do not agree with his Cal.Const. amend.chap.85. § § 221.5 (a)(b)(c)(d)(e)(f) ,for now as we have seen that his hate to God and conservative Christians who would disagree with him in this case is the biggest form is discrimination and bullying by a Governor of a State.

There is a lot of facts that prove it is wrong for a human being to even wear the opposite genders (sexual orientation) clothing in public places or at all, for this is the wrong type of thinking and a liberal way of thinking that it is okay to wear the opposite's gender clothing. Again using a boy for example wanted to wear girls' clothing in public place like in a public school setting, and wanting to try and be a cheerleader or even wear a dress to prom or even another type of either out of school activity or in school activity.

It is defiantly wrong to even allow a boy for example to urinate in the girls' bathroom or locker room, or to even dress and change into girl Phy-ed uniform in order to partake in gym class. As a parent that is against this idea of for example a boy to urinate or to change in the girls' locker room or bathroom, just what is your feelings and just what would your reaction be if a boy had the permission like it says under Cal.Const. amend.chap.85. § §221.5(a)(b)(c)(d)(e)(f), and are you going to accept your daughter[s] to be viewed by a boy when she is changing showering, for she would have to expose herself to the boy because under Cal.Const. amend.chap.85. § § 221.5 (a)(b)(c)(d)(e)(f) says it is okay and the liberals and democrats say you must and it is a mandate that a boy for example can view a girl in the nude and he can shower with the girls because Cal.Const. amend.chap.85. § § 221.5 (a)(b)(c)(d)(e)(f) say you have allow the boys to shower and urinate with your daughters. Now it is you as a parent that said it is okay because of what the liberals and democrats especially Governor Jerry Brown of California has mandated your sons to do this very thing. All of this is in the name of equality to be equal, and believe this that equality is not true equal rights. True equality is everyone is the same just like communism is all about.

Governor Jerry Brown has mandated that in the name of equality in the State of California that gender (Sexual Orientation) is no more, for a male is to be classified as a female. With that said Governor Jerry Brown has said that every female is a male too. If you disagree with that idea well you should review Cal.Const. amend.chap.85. § § 221.5 (a)(b)(c)(d)(e)(f) also you should review the U.S.Const. amend. XIV, for this is the United States Constitution whereby the ones like liberal democrat Governor Jerry Brown, President Obama, and Wisconsin's United States Senator Tammy Baldwin use in the name of equality to be equal.

U.S.Const.amend. XIV "Section 1.All persons born or naturalized in the United States, and subject to the jurisdiction thereof, are citizens of the United States and of the State wherein they reside. No State shall make or enforce any law which shall abridge the privileges or immunities of citizens of the United States; nor shall any State deprive any person of life, liberty, or property, without due process of law; nor deny to any person within its jurisdiction the equal protection of the laws. Section 2. Representatives shall be apportioned among the several States according to their respective numbers, counting the whole number of persons in each State, excluding Indians not taxed. But when the right to vote at any election for the choice of electors for President and Vice-President of the United States, Representatives in Congress, the Executive and Judicial officers of a State, or the members of the Legislature thereof, is denied to any of the male inhabitants of such State, being twenty-one years of age,* and citizens of the United States, or in any way abridged, except for participation in rebellion, or other crime, the basis of representation therein shall be reduced in the proportion which the number of such male citizens shall bear to the whole number of male citizens twenty-one years of age in such State. Section 3. No person shall be a Senator or Representative in Congress, or elector of President and Vice-President, or hold any office, civil or military, under the United States, or under any State, who, having previously taken an oath, as a member of Congress, or as an officer of the United States, or as a member of any State legislature, or as an executive or judicial officer of any State, to support the Constitution of the United States, shall have engaged in insurrection or rebellion against the same, or given aid or comfort to the enemies thereof. But Congress may by a vote of two-thirds of each House, remove such disability. Section 4.The validity of the public debt of the United States, authorized by law, including debts incurred for payment of pensions and bounties for services in suppressing insurrection or rebellion, shall not be questioned. But neither the United States nor any State shall assume or pay any debt or obligation incurred in aid of insurrection or rebellion against the United States, or any claim for the loss or emancipation of any slave; but all such debts, obligations and claims shall be held illegal and void. Section 5. The Congress shall have the power to enforce, by appropriate legislation, the provisions of this article." Now this Amendment to the United States Constitution is more or less for the employment of human beings in the United States of America and how a human being is to be treated under the law[s].

The Gender(Sexual Orientation) of a Human Being is determined in Its Mother Womb.

There is no real proof, facts, truths that can even backup the claim that either a boy or girl was born with the wrong gender (sexual orientation) like all liberals and democrats would like to believe.

In truth liberals and democrats cannot even understand the growth and development of a child that is in it mother's womb, for they have no faith in Truth, and Truth is the only one that determines the gender makeup in the mother's womb of a child, for all children be lone to Truth and only Truth. It would be true that all liberals and democrats hate Truth and will always hate Truth, for they just do not know Truth and do not even want to know or understand Truth.

According to Truth a child in its mother's womb has their gender determined at the time of conception and if the gender of a child is a male therefore that child will always be a male no matter what the liberals and democrats say and the law[s] the liberals and democrats would like to see on the books as law[s]; therefore the male in their mother womb is who he is and will stay that way, for there is no way to change the gender of the male that is in its mother's womb no matter what.

The government cannot make law[s] that would say it is okay for example boy to say he is a girl after he is born, for the boy is a boy at the time the sperm is received in the egg when conception has been formed; therefore boys you are a male and girls you are all females. The government has no unalienable right to say otherwise because the government tis not the Creator as it says in U.S. Declaration of Independence, Paragraph 2 (1776). The government cannot take the child away from their parents if the child has said no to being call another gender other than the gender at the time is conserved in its mother's womb, nor at the time of the birth of the child. The government must not even mandate, make it mandatory, force, or put any human being under the control of the government[s], court[s], law[s] to even violate the rights and will of any and all parents, groups, or organizations that go against the idea that the gender of a child can be determined after the birth of the child or even while the child in still being developed in its mother womb.

There is a very and defiant difference between a female and male, for in order to replenish the human pollution there has to be both males and females; therefor the government, and the parents, nor can a child can determine the gender of a child can be after birth.

So liberals, and democrats just who can determine the gender of a child according to the liberals and democrats? None of the liberals or democrats have it correct, for none and none of the liberals and democrats have the right to teach a child the fact that a child can have the right to make a choice or to determine just which gender the child would like to be or feel like.

To try to convince a child that they have the right[s] to say that they are born the wrong gender is immoral, and immorally insane, and all liberals and democrats that are willing to say these things are the ones that are immoral and immorally insane. This would include psychology, sociology, and other non-scientist like these groups, plus any parents to the child as well, including the government[s] that are not a conservative type of government[s].

It is immoral and immorally wrong for the parents of the child to determine and raise or develop a child as the opposite gender that the child is when if it formed, and developing in its mother's womb; therefore if the parents or a parent of the child even for example wants to raise the male child as a female child, that is immoral and immorally insane and very wrong to do, for that is a male child and must be raised as a male child. The same would go if a female child was born as a female, for she should never be raised as a male to get her to think she is a male.

To teach transgender is normal way of life is very immoral, and to teach that for example that a boy was born in the wrong body is immoral, plus there is no real proofs, facts, or any truth that all liberals and democrats can come up with, for all those that are in love with the idea of the immorality of transgender is an lie or fabrication made up by psychology with is a religion in truth, for the truth according to the definition of psychology is from Psychology Today, The Study of the Soul "The word psychology comes from the Greek psukhe, meaning "soul," "spirit," https://www.psychologytoday.com/blog/psychedelic-healing/201011/psychology-the-study-the-soul The fact even the (Psychology Today) even defines psychology is not a science at all, for the meaning from (psychology Today), and the Greek is the only way to even define the word psychology. Liberals and democrats do not like this definition, for all liberals and democrats would say this is the study of the mind, and there is no soul or spirt of a human being. Yet there is a soul and spirt of a human being, because we human beings are all created the same as the Truth.

Fact is and the proof is there is no science that can even prove (2014), Kathy/ canyonwalker connections, http://canyonwalkerconnections.com/sexual-orientation-and-science-hands/ "It does not matter that heterosexual do not make choices for sexual orientation; the argument is that glbt people somehow do. Proponents of "being gay is a choice."

Is that very interesting that being a LGBT, gay, homosexual, cross-dresser, same-sex person, etc. as a choice, but a heterosexual person has no choice at all to make; therefore a transgender person has made their choice outside of their mother's womb to which gender they are to be when the rest cannot even make a choice at all. Note that this is not even equality, for this would mean that a transgender person has more rights than a heterosexual person that was born either a male or female in their mother's womb.

What is being said here is that science has never and will never come up with any proofs, facts, or a truth to even back up the claim that the gender of a person can be wrong in the mother's womb, and the fact that God has made a mistake when it comes to the determining facts to the gender of a person in its mother's womb. By saying God has made a mistake is wrong way of thinking, for God cannot make any mistakes at all, for He is pure and Holly.

It also means that a person has to be taught to be gay, transgender, LGBT, homosexual, cross-dresser, or a person that would happen to agree with the liberals, democrats with this very interesting idea that a person is born this way etc… This also means is that all liberals, democrats are teaching idea that a person is a transgender, gay, LBGT, Homosexual, etc., in their mother's womb, with the help of psychology which is a religion that does not believe in God, for seeing that psychology is just a philosophy, and according to the definition of philosophy "anything or anyone with just an idea, theory, is just a religion with the exception of Christianity, and Jewish Church, for Christianity and Judaism is not a religion which the exception of a liberal Christianity because a liberal cannot be a christian, for a liberal Christian has no faith in Jesus Christ as their Lord and personal Savor at all, because a liberal christian has gone against the teaching that come from God. God is not a religion that is why Judaism and Christianity is not a religion like the secular worldview and the enemies against God would like everyone to believe. Liberals and democrats want everyone to believe that pure and true Christianity and Judaism is a religion that need to be deal with, by put those who believe to death. This means every human being that happens to believe in pure Christianity and Judaism put to death by the liberals and democrats.

What evidence, proofs, facts, or even a truth does the liberals, democrats have in the idea of a person gender is determined after that person is born? None for if they the liberals and democrats even want to make a law[s] like the Cal. Const. amend.chap.85. § § 221.5 (a)(b)(c)(d)(e)(f), or even any same-sex marriage law[s] and all in the name of equality, well just where is the equality in the fact that in (2014), Kathy/ canyonwalker connections, http://canyonwalkerconnections.com/sexual-orientation-and-science-hands/ "It does not matter that heterosexual do not make choices for sexual orientation; the argument is that glbt people somehow do. Proponents of "being gay is a choice." Does say there is no equality and not one person can even be equal when all homosexuals, LGBT, gay cross-dresser, transgender person, etc. has more special rights v. a heterosexual, and why is a heterosexual more hate group of people by the liberals, and democrats than a person with a different skin color? What unalienable right[s] is there in the name of equality and justice is there for a heterosexual?

In truth a boy is born as a male only and a girl is born as a female only, for there is no other way that it is possible, for a male to be born in the wrong body or a female to be born in the wrong body. Where is the proof?

Cal. Const. amend.chap.85. § § 221.5 (a)

Cal. Const. amend.chap.85. § § 221.5 (a) "(a) It is the policy of the state that elementary and secondary school classes and courses, including nonacademic and elective classes and courses, be conducted, without regard to the sex of the pupil enrolled in these classes and courses."

The first thing and fact with the proof and truth is the direct and willful violate of U.S.Const. amend. I "Congress shall make no law respecting an establishment of religion, or prohibiting the free exercise thereof; or abridging the freedom of speech, or of the press; or the right of the people peaceably to assemble, and to petition the government for a redress of grievances."

Governor Jerry Brown has willfully violated U.S.Const.amend. I by signing this into law and making an establishment of religion in the area that Governor Jerry Brown because of the fact is that a church school, or a church Sunday school that would happen to disagree with a boy for example wearing girls' clothing, cross-dressing, LGBT, gay, same-sex marriage, homosexuality, incest, bestiality, liberal idea of religion, the rights of those who wish to worship God as they feel home school, charter school, choice school, for according to Governor Jerry Brown not one human being has the right of religion unless he says it is okay according to his views of how one is to worship God, or any false god that is out there, and not just in the State of California, but in every State in the nation. Any and all liberals that agreed with Governor Jerry Brown is also in violation of U.S.Const.amend.I just like Governor Jerry Brown and so are all the democrats and republicans that voted in favor of this part of the law too. With all of that stated it is even clear that Governor Jerry Brown has directly, willfully, violated this part of U.S.Const.amend.I "prohibiting the free exercise thereof ", for all types of churches, church schools, church Sunday school, Bible Studies, home school, charter school, choice school, private schools, republicans, other political groups that are conservative, Pastor, Priest, lay leader of a church, parents, or anyone that happens to disagree with Cal. Const. amend.chap.85.§ § 221.5 (a)(b)(c)(d)(e)(f)

and Governor Jerry Brown, or the liberal worldview cannot say anything at all for those who do are in direct violation of Cal. Const. amend.chap.85.§ § 221.5 (a)(b)(c)(d)(e)(f) and Governor Gary Brown of the State of California even those from different States in the Union too.

This part of U.S.Const.amend I "or abridging the freedom of speech", is also a direct, willfully, violation that Governor Jerry Brown, and liberals with the help of all democrats and the republicans that sided with these type of people as well. It was noted this in the about part this thesis, for the fact and proof is Governor Jerry Brown of the State of California in truth is saying that every individual has no rights under Cal. Const. amend.chap.85.§ § 221.5 (a)(b)(c)(d)(e)(f) and §(a) does point this fact out to be truth, for if anyone in the United States of

America says anything at all against Governor Jerry Brown of the State of California or the Cal. Const. amend.chap.85.§ § 221.5 (a)(b)(c)(d)(e)(f) , or if a boy wants to cross-dress or to just say he is a girl that day, or even prohibits him to partake in a church whereby a church is against his desire to wear female clothing such as for example a dress, or the same in a private school, home school, charter school, choice school, church Sunday school, Bible study, etc., would have no more freedom of speech, and this would be found to be truth according to §(a) of Const. amend.chap.85.§ § 221.5 (a)(b)(c)(d)(e)(f).

Seeing that Governor Jerry Brown of the State of California has also violated U.S.Const.amend. I in the "the right of the people peaceably to assemble". Now according to Governor Jerry Brown and the democrats with the liberals are saying that a church, private school, home school, charter school, choice school, church Sunday school, Bible study, etc., family that is against Governor Jerry Brown or the liberals democrats, or anyone that is against the idea of Const. amend.chap.85.§ § 221.5 (a)(b)(c)(d)(e)(f) especially§(a) cannot assemble peacefully unless there is a boy that thinks he is a girl, or wants to cross-dress if he chooses too. A church cannot even preach the truth, for the Truth is against the law known as the Const. amend.chap.85.§ § 221.5 (a)(b)(c)(d)(e)(f) and all liberals and anyone that happens to agree with Governor Jerry Brown and the democrats, liberals, and all those that agree with Const. amend.chap.85.§ § 221.5 (a)(b)(c)(d)(e)(f) or any and all law[s] that are connected to this law.

The second fact and proof is that every boy for example would be required to cross-dress, and to be established to have their identification as a male removed and be forced, mandated, or have it mandatory to be identified as a transgendered female or a female as their gender identification . Now if the boy or the parents of the boy does not agree with this idea or part of the law that is Cal. Const. amend.chap.85. § § 221.5 (a)(b)(c)(d)(e)(f) they would be in direct violation of Cal. Const. amend.chap.85. § § 221.5 (a)(b)(c)(d)(e)(f). A school uniform must be required that would have to state that all boys no matter what would have to comply with a school uniform code that comes the school district that they happen to live that all boys would be forced, mandate or it would be mandatory for a boy to wear a dress or if the school uniform is a skirt, blouse all female undergarments that are a requirement even if the school in the school district is a church school, church Sunday school, private school, choice school, charter school, Bible study, etc. This would also include that all athletics programs would have to mandate, force, or even make it mandatory that all boys must even wear the uniforms that a girl would in their phy-ed class this would include swimming classes, diving course. It would be truth that under § (a) that all boys would have to be mandated, forced, or a mandatory swim suit that a female would have wear all boys must wear the same as a female would.

All boys would have to make themselves look like a female at all cost to them and be forced not to own, buy any male clothing just to comply with Cal. Const. amend.chap.85. § § 221.5 (a) whether they happen to disagree with Governor Jerry Brown and the forced not to own, buy any male clothing just to comply with Cal. Const. amend.chap.85. § § 221.5 (a)(b)(c)(d)(e)(f), plus the parent of the boy that would happen to disagree with this law could be punished for even thinking or violating this law or both the boy[s] and their parents.

Also and according to § (a) if there is no boy that is willing to partake in a nonacademic program for example as a cheerleader; boy[s] could be forced, mandated or have it mandatory to be a cheerleader and wear the very same cheerleader uniform as a girl cheerleader would. This idea could include all female sports and sporting events too.

Cal. Const. amend.chap.85. § § 221.5 (b)

Cal. Const. amend.chap.85. § § 221.5(b) "A school district may not prohibit a pupil from enrolling in any class or course on the basis of the sex of the pupil, except a class subject to Chapter 5.6 (commencing with Section 51930) of Part 28 of Division 4 of Title 2."

In § (b) would include all schools that are in any school that is in the State of California, for all schools are all under the control of the State government, for this is a mandatory mandate to have full control by the State government. All schools does mean church schools, private schools, charter schools, home schools, choice schools, ect.

The fact is § (b) is the very same as a communist nation would have set up all their school programs and school districts within the communist government. The language in § (b) is the same as liberals and democrats would us, for Governor Jerry Brown did agree to the same language as the communist would making the State of California a communist type of State that would have all its citizen now under a communist control type of government whereby not one citizen of the State of California has not right to say otherwise as it was talked about and written is the above section of this thesis. No more U.S.Const.amend. I that is what § (b) of Cal. Const. amend.chap.85. § § 221.5(a)(b)(c)(d)(e)(f) means.

Cal. Const. amend.chap.85. § § 221.5(c)

Cal. Const. amend.chap.85. § § 221.5(c) "(c) A school district may not require a pupil of one sex to enroll in a particular class or course, unless the same class or course is also required of a pupil of the opposite sex."

The wording and meaning in §(c) is the wording of a mandatory with mandate, or are

forced to do this would include all church school including a church Sunday school or Bible class or any other type of religion type of schools that would be against Governor Gary Brown and the Cal. Const. amend.chap.85. § § 221.5 (a)(b)(c)(d)(e)(f) especially §(c) this would include charter schools, private schools, choice schools, even all home schools, ect.

§(c) does back up both §(a) and §(b) that a mandatory mandate is made and has to be enforced by the Executive Branch of Government according to U.S.Const.art.II without §4 of U.S.Const.art.II, for §4 has to be and it needs to be eliminated before the liberal type of law like Cal. Const. amend.chap.85. § § 221.5 (a)(b)(c)(d)(e)(f) is to be enforced and dictated to the citizen of the State of California.

In §(c) all schools in the district would and must comply even if the school is a church schools, church Sunday schools or Bible classes, private schools, charter schools, choice schools, etc. cannot have any type of course or program that would be for just one gender only even an athletic program, and yes this means cheerleader, proms, school dances, any beauty contest or beauty pageants, All phy-ed, health class, shop class, home education class must be a coed type of class even if the class is designed for example an all-female class or a club or an group, or organization that would hold their meeting after school hour on a school campus. The true meaning is that there must be and it is a mandatory mandated, to be a force made by and according to the Cal. Const. amend.chap.85. § § 221.5 (a)(b)(c)(d)(e)(f) law.

Cal. Const. amend.chap.85. § § 221.5(d)

Cal. Const. amend.chap.85. § § 221.5(d) "(d) A school counselor, teacher, instructor, administrator, or aide may not, on the basis of the sex of a pupil, offer vocational or school program guidance to a pupil of one sex that is different from that offered to a pupil of the opposite sex or, in counseling a pupil, differentiate career, vocational, or higher education opportunities on the basis of the sex of the pupil counseled. Any school personnel acting in a career counseling or course selection capacity to a pupil shall affirmatively explore with the pupil the possibility of careers, or courses leading to careers, that are nontraditional for that pupil's sex. The parents or legal guardian of the pupil shall be notified in a general manner at least once in the manner prescribed by Section 48980, in advance of career counseling and course selection commencing with course selection for grade 7 so that they may participate in the counseling sessions and decisions."

Here are the words that are mandatory to be mandated and forces all parents or legal guardians that they have no legal rights at all how to raise their very own child or children in the area of education at all. "The parents or legal guardian of the pupil shall be notified in a general manner at least once in the manner prescribed by Section 48980, in advance of career counseling and course selection commencing with course selection for grade 7 so that they may participate in the counseling sessions and decisions." Governor Jerry Brown of the State of California wants to have everything mandatory with mandates in order for the government to be able to raise all children or a child. This very same idea is the ideas of a liberal or a democrat which is taken from the communistic type of government. One should point out that this would include all church schools, church Sunday schools, Bible class, private schools, charter schools, choice schools, etc. this would also mean if a child is to become a Pastor of a church, or if a child wants to become a church Sunday school teacher. Only the Government can be the only one to determine what a child is to do as a career and not the parents or legal guardian of a child.

All of this does mean that there are no rights according to the U.S.Const.amend. I; therefore the meaning is that Governor Jerry Brown of California is the only one that will decide who will do what as long as it does not violate the civil rights of all homosexuals, LGBT, gays, cross-dresser, transgender people, and other liberals that happen to agree with the Cal. Const. amend.chap.85. § § 221.5 (a)(b)(c)(d)(e)(f) law that he signed into law in 2013. A heterosexual has no rights according to §(c) of the Cal. Const. amend.chap.85. § § 221.5 (a)(b)(c)(d)(e)(f) which was signed into law by liberal democratic Governor Jerry Brown of California in 2013.

There are several places in history whereby there is real facts, proofs, and truth that would show the Cal. Const. amend.chap.85. § § 221.5 (a)(b)(c)(d)(e)(f) is a produce and law that comes from the communist, for if one just happen to read the book by Karl Marx the (Communist Manifesto) one would see the Cal. Const. amend.chap.85. § § 221.5 (a)(b)(c)(d)(e)(f) law in that book. One would also be able to read from the book by Karl Marx these words in the book that Governor Jerry Brown of California like to see like these words, mandatory, mandate, control, requirement. Also Adolf Hitler use the very same idea from 1933 to 1945 as well in Germany. In both nations there was no parental or legal guardian rights at all. Always keep in mind to study history for history will show what is in this thesis is the truth and only the truth.

Seeing that Governor Jerry Brown of the State of California has agreed to go the very same thing as the liberal idea by saying it is in the name of equality is insane and immoral, for he is saying that no parent[s] or legal guardian[s] would even have a moral right to disagree with him for Governor Jerry Brown of the State of California has made an executive decision to keep all parent[s] or legal guardian[s] out of the right to decide how their child is to educated, by saying only school counselor, teacher, instructor, administrator, or aide may not, on the basis of the sex of a pupil, offer vocational or school program guidance to a pupil of one sex that is different from that offered to a pupil of the opposite sex or, in counseling a pupil, differentiate career, vocational, or higher education opportunities on the basis of the sex of the pupil counseled. Any school personnel acting in a career counseling or course selection capacity to a pupil shall affirmatively explore with the pupil the possibility of careers, or courses leading to careers, that are nontraditional for that pupil's sex. Another words a stranger[s] or a liberal[s] can determine just a child is to do and just how the care of the child is to be.

Cal. Const. amend.chap.85. § § 221.5(e)

Cal. Const. amend.chap.85. § § 221.5(e) ".(e) Participation in a particular physical education activity or sport, if required of pupils of one sex, shall be available to pupils of each sex."

This part of Cal. Const. amend.chap.85. § § 221.5 (a)(b)(c)(d)(e)(f) does promote rape, immoral sexual activity, perversion, child pornography, and everything of immoral behaviour that all liberals, and democrats would love to see happen. This part of the law also takes away the separation between a girls' bathroom and boys' bath room, boys' locker room or changing room and a girls' locker room or changing room. By Governor Jerry Brown of the State of California signing Cal. Const. amend.chap.85. § § 221.5 (a)(b)(c)(d)(e)(f) in law and now must enforce Cal. Const. amend.chap.85. § § 221.5 (a)(b)(c)(d)(e)(f) is stating that he wants every boy or girl to see the other in the nude, and it is okay for either a boy or girl to see the opposite gender person nude whether the opposite gender object to them be seen nude or not.

Parent[s] or legal guardian[s] cannot even object to having either their son or daughter private body parts being viewed or seen by the person of the opposite gender, for now the students must share the very same locker rooms or changing rooms or even use the same bath rooms. Yes the words "Participation in a particular physical education activity or sport" is very clear here, but seeing if just for example a boy has it made mandatory, mandated, forced, to be a cheerleader whereby this activity is for girls' only, that boy would have to change in the girls' locker room or changing room with the girls' at the same time, and it would have to do with the idea of equality making the boy to be required to change at the same time because according to the liberals equall rights means all have the right to be at the same place at the same time, or else it is not equall under the law[s]. Liberals and democrats demand equality no matter what a person's gender is: therefore according to the liberals and democrats any boy has the civil right[s] to be able to change in the girls' locker room or changing room if they want to, and view a person of the opposite gender if they would like under Cal. Const. amend.chap.85. § § 221.5(e). Governor Jerry Brown of the State of California has made it legal for a person of the opposite gender to do so. Here is one thing that is true that cheerleading as a cheerleader is a physical education activity; therefore a boy must be a cheerleader if he want to be a cheerleader or not, and it is the choice that has to be made not by his parent[s] or legal guardian[s], but it is the choice that can be made by a school counselor, teacher, instructor, administrator, or aide, for all of the decision making is to be made this way according to§(d) of Cal. Const. amend.chap.85. § § 221.5 (a)(b)(c)(d)(e)(f) meaning a parent[s] or legal guardian[s] to have no right[s] according to the law.

Cal. Const. amend.chap.85. § § 221.5(f)

Cal. Const. amend.chap.85. § § 221.5(f) "(f) A pupil shall be permitted to participate in sex-segregated school programs and activities, including athletic teams and competitions, and use facilities consistent with his or her gender identity, irrespective of the gender listed on the pupil's records."

Sex-segregation does mean the very same thing as school-segregation from the 1960's and 1970's whereby black and white children are mandatory, mandate, or forced to go to the same school even if that means spending taxpayers' money to bus a child from one school to another from another school district or another part of that State just to please a minority, and all in the name of equality even if the parent[s] or legal guardian[s] of that child would even dare to object to this idea. Now the real problem is that the all liberals and all democrats love to see taxes go up and up just to support their agenda of making the United States of America as a communist nation. The same idea is with making it mandatory, a mandate, or even force with sex- segregation in any school even all private schools, church schools, church Sunday schools, Bible studies, charter schools, choice schools, home schools, ect... A home school would or could have children or the opposite sex or gender learning together, a private school could or would have both male and female students, and this requirement would have to be enforced by the Governor of the State of California. Church schools would or could have both male and female students and the same thing that seeing this would be a segregated school with both male and female students in the church school as well. In addition a church school could or would have athletic teams and competitions school programs and activities too, and the Governor of the State of California would have to and be forced to enforce Cal. Const. amend.chap.85. § § 221.5(f). Even if the church school does not allow any transgendered students in their schools, or even any and all homosexual students, LGBT students, gay student, Students of incest, or even disagrees with same-sex marriage too. The rule of having separate school programs and activities, including athletic teams and competitions in a church school is all based on Truth and moral way of living and standards of teachings of morality that comes from Truth and the way Truth teaches. A church School would have the right[s] to teach the way it feel fit to teach even having both male and females in separated class rooms if need be. This part of Cal. Const.

amend.chap.85. § § 221.5 (a)(b)(c)(d)(e)(f) is a direct deliberate violation of U.S.Const.amend.I whereby a church school would have the right to teach that a male and female student must have all separate facilities, and separate school programs and activities, including athletic teams and competitions even for example if a boy thinks he is a female and wants to identify himself as a female and the same goes for a girl if she thinks she is a male. A church school is a private school that is not supported by taxpayer money at all and has the "Unalienable Right[s]" to determine its very own rule and regulations; therefore the government[s] must stay out and never have the right to even control all and every school that is a church school no matter what. It is for this reason is why a church school is to be allowed in the United States of America and it does fall under this law as well. The law is found in the Johnson C. (1994-2013) MayflowerHistory.com. Retrieved from http://mayflowerhistory.com/mayflower-compact/.

The United States of America was founded on the very same principle as it is written in the Mayflower Compact of 1620, for it was religious freedom and the choice to be free to worship and teach the children of the United States of America the Truth about Truth as they felt fit to do and the way each church group of organization felt a child is to be taught, and not the government, King, Empire, or a Dictator wanted a child to be taught. Even the U.S. Declaration of Independence, Paragraph 2 (1776) and the U.S.Const. amend. I will back up just what the Mayflower Compact of 1620 does state of proof, facts, and truth to why separation is a necessary fact, proof, and truth is a must in every class room, school programs and activities, including athletic teams and competitions, and use facilities cannot be segregated, but remain separated to the gender of the child. This is why sex-segregation is just a term that all liberals and democrats love to use and say there must be in all schools no matter what. The government is not the church, but the church is the government, for government comes from the church, for the church is a family and the family is the smallest form of government; therefore the church is the government. Governor Jerry Brown of California is not the head of the church nor any church school, for he is not the head or above Truth. Even the communist found out that they are not above or the head of the church or even better than Truth; therefore all liberals and democrats will fail in what they do or think.

Irrespective of gender listed on the pupil's records would mean that without regard to something else would be the best way to say Governor Jerry Brown of the States of California has no regards to the fact that what is on the student[s] records as to their identity does not count and could be wrong, for Governor Jerry Brown does not like the real differences that does separate just what is the makeup of what is the difference between a male and female. It would also very clear that Governor Jerry Brown of the State of California is saying that a child after they are born can be the only one to determine just what gender there are to be no matter what the gender of the child is in its mother's womb, for according to what Governor Jerry Brown of the State of California has said that a child in its mother's womb has no gender identification at the time of conception. Governor Jerry Brown has no respect at all to any and all human beings. Thus the liberals and democrats can be said to be the same as Governor Jerry Brown of the State of California and would happen to agree with him 100% of the time.

There is a huge difference between the gender of a male and the gender of a female, for it is truth that there is no equality between a male and female when it comes to gender identification. It is very clear when a human being looks at just what is the real hard evidence and proof that would separate a male from a female is the fact is a male's body parts the physical ones are different than a female's body parts. So segregation would not even work like Governor

41

Gary Brown of the State of California and the liberals and democrats would like to see and say. A boy should not change clothing, use the same bath room or shower with a girl when it comes to school programs and activities, including athletic teams and competitions, and use facilities. Separate athletic teams and competitions, and use facilities and school programs is the only way to go when it comes to the safety of a student, and it does not support any sexual activity that would happen if there is a segregation between both male and female students.

Separation means freedom and liberty everything else would mean slavery and communism for the State of California and the rest of the nation.

A boy is a male and a girl is a female:

All boys are males and all girls are females at the time they are conception, and there is or should never be any way to change that, for it is wrong to tell a boy that he is a girl at the time of his conception, and it is wrong to tell a girl she is a boy at her time of conception too.

A boy does not have a vaginia at the time he is conceived in his mother's womb, nor he will never develop breast like a girl would at the time of puberty; therefore those who claim otherwise would be wrong to even tell a boy that he is a girl at the time he was conceived in his mother's womb; therefore a girl at the time of her conception will not be born with a penis, nor should be told it is okay for her to have her vaginia turned into a penis and have it whereby she will never develop any breast like a girl should at the time of puberty. There are many other characters that would also show that are very different between a male and female, and a male cannot have the characters that a female would have, and a female cannot have the same characters that a male would have. So why does Governor Jerry Brown of the State of California

42

and the liberals alone with the democrats want to have with the idea that a boy for example is boy in the wrong body or has the wrong gender to be identified with. The very same thing would go for a girl as well.

The idea that one could commit to modulation of one's body is very immoral and immorally wrong, for that is just what the liberals and the democrats would like to do with the help of Governor Jerry Brown of the State of California want to see and do.

Transgender is a made up word used for the liberals and democrats and men like Governor Gary Brown so that they can be like the other made up term that the liberals and democrats like to use so that they can have equality and the made up word is "politically correctness". This fact is truth that all liberals and democrats love to makeup these types of words or terms just to please themselves in order to make it hard to even disagree with them, or to makeup and hate crime law[s]. So a transgender boy is a made up phony word, and phony description of a boy that has been told by all liberals it is okay to be a girl. A transgender girl is a phony word or term just made up by the liberals and democrats just to please the girl that liberals and democrats like to call transgender. What is being said here all liberals and democrats love to tell lies just to please themselves and to get people to agree with them and their phony ideas.

To change how to identify either a boy or a girl is in truth very immoral, and is immorality to force other to do just that. For example if a boy thinks he was to be born a girl and the liberals and democrats with the help of Governor Jerry Brown the Governor of the State of California is showing not just the State of California how these people feel and think about things that are immoral, but they are the people that are promoting thinks that are immoral and saying all immorality is to become legal.

Boys and men must never wear any female clothing at all, for it is immoral and there is no morality or decency and it is a shame to see a boy or man wearing female clothing such as a dress or skirt.

Girls and all females should never wear or be seen wearing any and all male or boys clothing, for it is no morality or decency and it is a shame to see a girl wearing any and all clothing for a male to wear, and for all adult females should never wear any and all clothing that is for a male only.

Conclusion:

Cal. Const. amend.chap.85. § § 221.5 (a)(b)(c)(d)(e)(f) is wrong, for there is no freedom and liberty with this law, for it does remove the right[s] of a parent[s] or legal guardian[s] of a child to the right to raise and teach the child as they fell fit to do so. A child or student would no longer have any right[s] that are in the Constitution of the United States of America as well as the parent[s] or legal guardian[s] of the child or student. It very clear that the liberals and democrats with the help of Governor Jerry Brown of the State of California want to eliminate all freedom and all liberty of the parent[s] or legal guardian[s] of how to educate and raise a child or student[s], plus have all immorality to be legal and to eliminate morals and all morality of life.

Cal. Const. amend.chap.85. § § 221.5 (a)(b)(c)(d)(e)(f) is a direct violation of U.S.Const.amend.I, U.S. Declaration of Independence, Paragraph 2 (1776) as well as U.S.Const. amend. I, Cal.Fam.Code §7500 §(a)(b)(c), CAL.FAM.CODE § 7501§(a)(b),Cal.Fam.Code.

§7002 or even the identification of a male human being or a female human being. This violation is one that comes from the liberals, democrats, and Governor Jerry Brown of the State of California. It is this very reason why it is so important to note that no government or individual has the right to enslave another human being like the liberals and democrats love to do like Governor Jerry Brown of the State of California would like to do or has done so far, and make what is immoral and against all morality to even be legal.

Governor Jerry Brown of the State of California alone with the liberals and democrats have no right to make all immorality and immoral things legal or to force them onto any other human being or make that immoral immorality a part of religion. In order to do this that means with the proofs, facts and truths that have been brought forward in this thesis does show in order to allow what is immorality as a legal part of the law[s] means that what is moral and morality has to be made as illegal. We have seen this to be truth in histories past from the communist and socialist which are all haters of all things both moral and morality.

Governor Jerry Brown of the State of California, liberals, and democrat hate heterosexuals who are the majority of the voters in the State of California and in the United States of America, for in order to even state that transgender is a normal way of life is very wrong, for the transgender is just a less than one percent of the population of the State of California and the United States of America.

A church, church school, church Sunday school, or Bible study whereby a child is a student have the right to say how a child or student is to be taught alone with private schools, charter schools, choice schools, home schools, ect; therefore it is an unalienable right as well as an individual right to teach a child it is wrong to even be a transgender child, for the gender of a child is determined at the time of conception not after the birth of a child. Being homosexuality,

45

LGBT, gay, cross-dressing, being a cross-dresser and other forms of immorality like these are do not have to be taught by any group[s], organization[s], having it mandatory, mandated or even force upon by the government, liberals, democrats, or even Governor Jerry Brown of the State of California with any silly law[s] like the Cal. Const. amend.chap.85. § § 221.5 (a)(b)(c)(d)(e)(f) law is all about. Being immoral like the homosexuals are, LGBT, gays, cross-dressers, boys' thing that they are in the wrong body and the same would go for a girl to think that way too are all immoral too.

The fact is for an example is that a boy for example could fake could state that he feels like he is a girl like a transgendered boy would do and in truth commit an immoral crime of peeking at girls going to the bath room, or changing in the girls locker room or changing room, and not even be punished for the crime[s] in which he has committed. This is why there is no such thing as a transgendered person at all. Transgender is just a made up ward by the liberals and democrats like to do a lot, in addition what a liberal and democrats is truthfully saying is that everyone must be what is called politically correct in order to have the immoral words tolerance and diversity, for all liberals and democrats just love to have everything immoral legal, and everything that is moral illegal. Governor Jerry Brown of the State of California is one of many that are a lover of immorality and other immoral words. The truth about this one fact is that Governor Jerry Brown of California did sign Cal. Const. amend.chap.85. § § 221.5 (a)(b)(c)(d)(e)(f) into law and sided with immorality to be immoral without knowing the fact or he just did not even care to listen to the facts, or did not even want to know the facts.

Now after reviewing the law inclusion this fact does run to be truth as well whereby now the government of the State of California and any other place such as a city could use the law to even force for example that all boys or even adult males must have it mandatory, mandated, or even forced by law[s] to wear female clothing like a dress, or and all males no matter of their age

are to be even have it made mandatory, mandated, forced, required to no longer wear male

clothing, but are to wear female clothing, or female clothing will be the only type of clothing that

can be bought or sold to the general public whether the persons agrees or not. This can be found

in words that are used example "segregation" which mean to be the same as; therefore the only

real acceptable gender would have to be a female for reason that just about everything is

designed around or for a female. This would be used for this term "gender equality" meaning

equal for all.

Boys and men must never wear any female clothing at all, for it is immoral and there is

no morality or decency and it is a shame to see a boy or man wearing female clothing such as a

dress or skirt.

Girls and all females should never wear or be seen wearing any and all male or boys

clothing, for it is no morality or decency and it is a shame to see a girl wearing any and all

clothing for a male to wear, and for all adult females should never wear any and all clothing that

is for a male only.

The Cal. Const. amend.chap.85. § § 221.5 (a)(b)(c)(d)(e)(f) is a law that would enforce

all immoral and immorality to be legal and those things that are moral and morality is to be now

illegal in the State of California, and other places that happen to adapt this illegal law as part of

their law[s]. This does answer the very question to what is wrong with Cal. Const.

amend.chap.85. § § 221.5 (a)(b)(c)(d)(e)(f)? the answer is immoral and immorality and

everything that goes with immoral and immorality. There is a huge difference between a male

and female when it comes down to certain things in both physical and mental development and abilities. There is no equality when it comes to a male or female. Equality is just wishful thinking by all liberals and democrats including Governor Jerry Brown of the State of California.

Cal. Const. amend.chap.85. § § 221.5 (a)

Cal. Const. amend.chap.85. § § 221.5 (a) "(a) It is the policy of the state that elementary and secondary school classes and courses, including nonacademic and elective classes and courses, be conducted, without regard to the sex of the pupil enrolled in these classes and courses."

This part of the law does indicate this truth to be true, for when Governor Jerry Brown of the State of California is stating that the rule of communism is the rule of law or is freedom no longer to be part of all those that live or visit the State of California, for now Governor Jerry Brown of the State of California has to answer if this is so just by signing this into law.

As it is written in this part of the Cal. Const. amend.chap.85. § § 221.5 (a)(b)(c)(d)(e)(f), in §(a) does show to be a mandatory, mandate, requirement, force, for "It is the policy of the State" that all types of schools no matter if the school is a public school or a church, church school, church Sunday school, private school, choice school, charter school, home school, and would even include any type of school that is not listed are all mandatory, mandate, requirement, force to comply with this part of the law according to Governor Jerry Brown of the State of California and the rest of the liberals and democrats.

If for example if the sex of the pupil is a male then everything; therefore all course that are for a male must and should remain for the male only, and a female must not be allowed in any school classes and courses, including nonacademic and elective classes and courses that is for a male student only.

In §(a) does show all parent[s] and legal guardian[s] have no legal right[s] to how they can even raise their own child that they feel if to, and the State of California according to Governor Jerry Brown has made it now and will enforce this part of the law to the effect that the States of California will be the one that has the right to raise the child as they feel fit even in the area of education.

Cal. Const. amend.chap.85. § § 221.5 (b)

Cal. Const. amend.chap.85. § § 221.5(b) "A school district may not prohibit a pupil from enrolling in any class or course on the basis of the sex of the pupil, except a class subject to Chapter 5.6 (commencing with Section 51930) of Part 28 of Division 4 of Title 2."
Seeing that a church, church school, church Sunday or Bible Study, private school, choice school, charter school, home school, and would even include any type of school that is not listed are all mandatory, mandate, requirement, force to comply with this part of the law according to Governor Jerry Brown of the State of California and the rest of the liberals and democrats not to prohibit a pupil from enrolling from any class or course on the basis of the sex of the pupil. Yet the one thing is these words in the law "A school district". The meaning of "A school district" is every school that is in that district which would include the following types of schools that would be found in the district. A church, church school, church Sunday or Bible Study, private school, choice school, charter school, home school, and would even include any type of school that is not listed are all mandatory, mandate, requirement, force to comply with this part of the law

49

according to Governor Jerry Brown of the State of California and the rest of the liberals and democrats. If a school of any type does not and has rejected or is willing to do what is called "civil disobedience" is to be forced by the liberals, democrats, and Governor Jerry Brown of the State of California would be force to force a pupil of the opposite gender in the class or course even if the school policy state no student of the opposite gender may take or enter the class or course of the opposite gender even if the parent[s] or legal guardian[s] would object to having the student in that class or course.

This is also a part of the law in which is the way of a communism type of government

and is away for the liberals and democrats to gain full control of all human life with the help of Governor Jerry Brown of the State of California. A clear violation of both human and unalienable right[s].

Cal. Const. amend.chap.85. § § 221.5(c)

Cal. Const. amend.chap.85. § § 221.5(c) "(c) A school district may not require a pupil of one sex to enroll in a particular class or course, unless the same class or course is also required of a pupil of the opposite sex."

Again there is the words "school district" meaning every school that exist in that one

single district no matter what type of school it maybe. The other word that is a mandatory, mandate, force, is the word require, for the word require does mean mandatory, mandate, force, ect., yet if the school is a church, church school, church Sunday or Bible Study, private school, choice school, charter school, home school, and would even include any type of school that is not listed that does not require a pulp of the opposite gender or will not allow a pulp of the opposite gender, for the school does believe in separation of the pulp with the opposite gender, then that school would have to be forced by the State of California and the law would have to be enforced by the Governor of the State of California Jerry Brown who is a liberal democrats that hates the words "separation of gender".

Cal. Const. amend.chap.85. § § 221.5(d)

Cal. Const. amend.chap.85. § § 221.5(d) "(d) A school counselor, teacher, instructor, administrator, or aide may not, on the basis of the sex of a pupil, offer vocational or school program guidance to a pupil of one sex that is different from that offered to a pupil of the opposite sex or, in counseling a pupil, differentiate career, vocational, or higher education opportunities on the basis of the sex of the pupil counseled. Any school personnel acting in a career counseling or course selection capacity to a pupil shall affirmatively explore with the pupil the possibility of careers, or courses leading to careers, that are nontraditional for that pupil's sex. The parents or legal guardian of the pupil shall be notified in a general manner at least once in the manner prescribed by Section 48980, in advance of career counseling and course selection commencing with course selection for grade 7 so that they may participate in the counseling sessions and decisions."

§(d) does keep all parent[s] and or legal guardian[s] from the right to raise their own children or child that is under their care even if the child was born in its own mother's womb. The one person that can or could even counsel a child is the "school counselor, teacher, instructor, administrator, or aide may not, on the basis of the sex of a pupil, offer vocational or school program guidance to a pupil." Which by the way is a stranger to the child; therefore a stranger of a child has more right[s] to help raise a child v. the parent[s] or legal guardian[s] of the child. The idea does come from the communist way of governing and this is very plain in

North Korea whereby the parent[s] or legal guardian[s] have no rights at all. All children according to the North Korean government does belong to the government. The Governor of California loves this idea of having the government own all students just the liberals and democrats do.

Cal. Const. amend.chap.85. § § 221.5(e)

Cal. Const. amend.chap.85. § § 221.5(e) ".(e) Participation in a particular physical education activity or sport, if required of pupils of one sex, shall be available to pupils of each sex."

Again this part of the law is geared to communism and the way the communist love to handle education of a child. A boy cannot play field hockey nor should that boy, for field hockey is a sport for females only. In addition there is no way a boy could wear the very same field hockey uniform as a female, because of the fact a boy's body design is very different that of a girl's is. A boy should never be forced into physical education activity or sport that is designed just for a female only, and the same for a female, for if a school such as a church school has separate physical education activity or sport for both the females and males then it should remain separated to as the school policy, and the doctrine of the church school, for the government would have no right[s] to force the church schools to even make it mandatory, mandate, required, forced to even change church doctrine in order to please the liberals. Other words a church school or church should not even have segregation of all pulps in order to please the government even if it does violate all church doctrine[s] at all. This very clear under U.S.Const.amend. I.

Cal. Const. amend.chap.85. § § 221.5(f)

Cal. Const. amend.chap.85. § § 221.5(f) "(f) A pupil shall be permitted to participate in sex-segregated school programs and activities, including athletic teams and competitions, and use facilities consistent with his or her gender identity, irrespective of the gender listed on the pupil's records."

Segregation is a word that comes from the communism way of life, and is a meaning that very one is to be the same; thus this is why all liberals and democrats alone with the Governor of the State of California Jerry Brown happen to agree that everyone must be segregated making everyone with the very same gender when in truth not one single human being that alive or now dead is even equal or has the same equality as another human being that is why each and every human being is created to be different than one another. This is why there should not be any sex-segregated school programs even in the area of athletics, and other types of competitions, and a pulp must never share the very same facilities like a bath room, locker room, or even a changing room. A male bath is for males only, and a females bath room is for females only, a males locker room is for males only, a females locker room is for females only likewise for changing rooms. Governor Jerry Brown of the State of California, liberals, and democrats cannot and under no circumstance force, make it mandatory, mandate, require, or force any and all pulps no matter what the gender of that child is to be segregated with the child of the opposite gender. Only a communist type of government would even segregate all children no matter what the gender of a child is.

Finally seeing that Governor Jerry Brown is a liberal democrat of the State of California he and he alone is to be held accountable, responsible, for the health and safety of all student[s] or pulps in every school and school district in the State of California whether he likes it or not.

Governor Jerry Brown who is a liberal democrat of the State of California cannot dictate or should never violate a law[s] like U.S.Const.amend.I, U.S. Declaration of Independence, Paragraph 2 (1776), or any and all moral law[s] and code[s] in which all law[s] are to be based on, and not to enforce all immoral law[s] and code[s] like the Cal. Const. amend.chap.85. § § 221.5(a)(b)(c)(d)(e)(f) is. To enforce all immoral law[s] based on the act of immorality is not what an executive branch of any and all governments are to do; therefore Cal. Const. amend.chap.85. § § 221.5(a)(b)(c)(d)(e)(f) is a violation of humanity; thus Governor Jerry Brown who is a liberal democrat of the State of California is the main and only causes behind hate crimes and is a lover of those things that force hate onto people that should never have any hate forced onto them, for all human being should have the right to live in peace, and not hate like Governor Jerry Brown who is a liberal democrat of the State of California wants with his Cal.Const. amend.chap.85. § § 221.5(a)(b)(c)(d)(e)(f). This is what is wrong with Cal.Const. amend.chap.85. § § 221.5(a)(b)(c)(d)(e)(f).

Bibliography

Cal. Const. amend.chap.85. § § 221.5(a)(b)(c)(d)(e)(f)

Cal. Const. amend.chap.85. § § 221.5(a)

Cal. Const. amend.chap.85. § § 221.5(b)

Cal. Const. amend.chap.85. § § 221.5(c)

Cal. Const. amend.chap.85. § § 221.5(d)

Cal. Const. amend.chap.85. § § 221.5(e)

Cal. Const. amend.chap.85. § § 221.5(f)

Cal.Fam.Code §7500 §(a)(b)(c)

CAL.FAM.CODE § 7501§(a)(b)

Cal.Fam.Code. §7002

State of California Head of Household (HOH) Legal Definitions under Qualifying

Child https://www.ftb.ca.gov/individuals/hoh/selftest/definitions.shtml#ParentStepparent

U.S.Const.amend.I

U.S.Const.amend.X

U.S.Const. amend. XIV

U.S. Declaration of Independence, Paragraph 2 (1776)

Johnson C. (1994-2013) MayflowerHistory.com. Retrieved from

http://mayflowerhistory.com/mayflower-compact/

Virgil T. (2014) "The Defense of Wisconsin Marriage Amendment 2006 (Thesis)

Psychology: The Study of the Soul https://www.psychologytoday.com/blog/psychedelic-

healing/201011/psychology-the-study-the-soul

(2014), Kathy/ canyonwalker connections, http://canyonwalkerconnections.com/sexual-orientation-and-science-hands/

www.ingramcontent.com/pod-product-compliance
Lightning Source LLC
Chambersburg PA
CBHW041508280526
45792CB00004B/1176